Lorenz Engel

Among the
PLAINS INDIANS

Lerner Publications Company
Minneapolis, Minnesota

The Library of Congress cataloged the original printing of this title as follows:

Engel, Lorenz.

Among the Plains Indians. [Text by Lor. Engel, photos by Heinz Binder, sketches by Heinz Giebeler. English translation by Susan W. Dickinson] Minneapolis, Lerner Publications Co. [1970, c1967]

112 p. illus. (part col.), col. map. 22 x 25 cm.

Describes briefly the way of life of various Plains Indians. Each descriptive passage is illustrated with a painting by Karl Bodmer or George Catlin.

Translation of Unter Indianern.

Includes illus. by George Catlin and Karl Bodmer.

1. Indians of North America—Pictures, illustrations, etc.—Juvenile literature. [1. Indians of North America] I. Catlin, George, 1796-1872, illus. II. Bodmer, Karl, 1809-1893, illus. III. Title.

E77.5.E513 1970	970.1	74-102895
ISBN 0-8225-0564-9		MARC
		AC

A NATURE AND MAN BOOK

Third Printing 1978

First published in the United States 1970 by Lerner Publications Company.
Minneapolis, Minnesota. All English language rights reserved.
Published simultaneously in Canada by J. M. Dent & Sons Ltd., Don Mills, Ontario.
Copyright © MCMLXVII by Deutsche Verlags-Anstalt, Stuttgart, Germany.

International Standard Book Number: 0-8225-0564-9
Library of Congress Catalog Card Number: 74-102895

Manufactured in the United States of America.

CONTENTS

INTRODUCTION

Thirty years after Lewis and Clark set out on their remarkable journey across the continent of North America, a group of Germans prepared an expedition which would follow in the earlier explorers' footsteps. In 1833, Alexander Phillip Maximilian, prince of the German principality of Wied, led a small party of explorers into the heart of the American wilderness. Maximilian was a scholar with a special interest in natural history. He took with him on his American expedition a young Swiss artist, Karl Bodmer, who was to make on-the-spot drawings and paintings to illustrate the published account of their travels. The prince and his companions journeyed for two years in the territory along the upper Missouri River. There were no large settlements of white people in this area, only scattered forts which served as outposts for United States Army units and meeting places for fur trappers and traders.

In the spring of 1833, when Maximilian and his companions were in St. Louis preparing for their trip, they saw a collection of oil paintings which pictured the country and people they were soon to see. The paintings had been done by the American artist, George Catlin, who had made an expedition along the upper Missouri only the year before. Catlin was fascinated by the Indians of the American plains; in addition to his travels in the Missouri valley, he made other trips among the Indians in Kansas, Oklahoma, and Minnesota, drawing and painting as he went. Like the prince and his party, Catlin became familiar with America's native population before it was forced aside by the white man's final conquest of the continent and totally changed by contact with his alien way of life.

Both Catlin and the Prince of Wied visited Indian settlements and hunting grounds which no white man had ever entered before. They were among the first visitors to this world who were not motivated by an idle thirst for adventure, a desire to conquer, or a need for land. The American artist and the German scholar wanted only to explore the territory in the interest of knowledge. Nevertheless, in spite of their peaceful intentions their travels were not without adventure and strain. Both expeditions brought back many important findings and records, but probably the most precious of all were the drawings and paintings done by the two artists. Without Bodmer's and Catlin's pictures we should not know today what life was like for the Plains Indians of the early 19th century.

Indian tribes had lived in North America for thousands of years before the white man arrived in the 16th century. The European settlement of the continent moved from east to west, gradually at first and then gathering momentum like an avalanche. The Indians lost their land, without which they could not live. They were forced westward, back across the continent in the direction from which they had originally come. As we can see from their appearance and from some of their tools, the Indians first came to North America from Asia during the Ice Age, when there was still land connecting Siberia and Alaska. They crossed the Bering Strait between 30,000 and 10,000 B.C., and by 8,000 B.C. they had spread throughout the continent.

There are only about 732,000 Indians in the United States and Canada today. Once, before the European settlers came, there were probably several million Indians, separated into many different tribes. Scholars often divide the original Indian population of the United States into five major culture groups; each group includes tribes which had a similar way of life and usually lived in a similar region of the country. The five culture groups or areas are: the Eastern Forest; the Plains; the Northwest Coast; the California-Intermountain area; and the Southwest. The languages of the North American Indians have been classified into about 50 different language families, each of which has a similar grammar and many words of similar origin. The language families of the most important Indian tribes are listed at the end of this book, together with a map showing the general location of each large language group.

Today many American Indians live far from their original homes in the continent's forests and prairies. Indian languages once spoken by thousands of people are now known to only a few. The world of the Plains Indians as it existed in the 19th century has been changed beyond recovery. However, by means of the story and pictures in this book we may regain some knowledge of that lost world and its inhabitants. The expedition described here is fictional, but it is based on the information gathered by Prince Maximilian and George Catlin and includes many of the characters and events mentioned in the accounts of their travels. The illustrations were selected from the lithographs in Catlin's *North American Indian Portfolio,* published in 1844, and from the volume of Bodmer's engravings which accompanied Maximilian's account of their expedition, *Reise in das Innere Nord-Amerikas in den Fahren 1832 bis 1834* (1839-1841).

Representatives of three tribes

In the spring of 1832, the members of the expedition assembled in St. Louis to prepare for their journey to the land of the Plains Indians. Here they had the good fortune to meet Indians from several different tribes which had sent delegations to visit the white man's cities. One of the delegates was an Iroquoi warrior (center) with long hair, feathered headdress, a ring through his nose, and a tomahawk in his hand. He came from an area east of the Great Lakes where the Iroquoi lived mainly by farming; they had formed a highly organized union of five tribes. The explorers also met an Osage Indian (left), whose tribe hunted on the prairies of Arkansas, Missouri, and Oklahoma. He was wearing a buffalo hide robe, leggings with scalping trophies, and a necklet of bears' claws. The scalp piece of hair on his half-shaved head was ornamented with deer hair. The Indian women in the delegations were dressed very simply, their plain outfits in sharp contrast to the colorful attire of the men. Among them was a Pawnee woman (right), whose people farmed maize (Indian corn) west of the Missouri River, in territory that later became the state of Nebraska.

George Catlin

10 Catching wild horses

Finally it was time for the expedition to begin.
The explorers left St. Louis and set out over
the plains of northern Missouri in the direction
of the Dakota territory. After traveling for
several days they came across a large herd of
wild horses out on the open prairie. These
animals were not native to North America; they
had been brought to Mexico by the Spanish
in the 16th century, and since that time wild
herds had gradually spread across the continent. As the explorers watched the horses from
a distance, they saw a group of riders approaching. The riders — they were Indians — gal-
loped toward the herd and tried to catch some
of the escaping animals with their swinging
lassos. One hunter succeeded in throwing
his lasso around the neck of a horse. Then
he let himself be dragged along by the terrified
animal until it dropped down, exhausted by the
choking effect of the rope. Quickly he threw
himself on the horse, tied its front legs, and
made a halter out of a small piece of rope. He
was now able to loosen the rope around the
animal's neck and pull at the halter with all
his might. The horse could get its breath back
and was able to stand up, yet it was still in
the hunter's power. The animal's breaking
and taming were now merely a question of time.

George Catlin

12 Hunting in animal disguise

One day, while the explorers were still crossing the endless prairie, one of them saw in the distance a grazing herd of bison — American buffalo. Through the prairie grass a number of wolves were moving towards the bison — no, not wolves, but Indians with wolf skins thrown over them! The hunters succeeded in coming quite close to the animals who felt safe in the herd and did not usually run away from wolves. Because of the buffalo's lack of fear the Indians were able to fire several fatal arrows at close range and to secure for themselves the meat and hides which were necessary for their survival. This dangerous method of hunting was often used by the prairie Indians before the horse was introduced as an animal for riding. Even after this time Indians who could not afford to own horses continued to hunt in animal disguise. When pursuing deer in this manner, the hunters either wore deer heads or covered themselves with whole deerskins.

George Catlin

Chief Mato-Tope

Gradually the party was approaching the territory of the Mandan Indians, a powerful and enterprising tribe which was known for its friendliness toward white people. The Mandan lived on the Missouri River in the Dakota territory, where the land was suitable for farming, and hunting provided an abundant source of food and clothing. Suddenly Indian scouts who had obviously been watching the strangers for a long time popped up out of the bushes, came nearer, and indicated that the strangers were expected. Soon there appeared a magnificently dressed warrior wearing a huge feather headdress and painted bison robe, his feet in embroidered moccasins. It was Mato-Tope, The Four Bears, one of the most accomplished Mandan warriors and second chief of the tribe. In a self-assured way he propped up his spear and welcomed the travelers, pointing to the nearby camp.

Karl Bodmer

The Mandan village

The path to Mih-Tutta-Hangkusch, the larger of the two Mandan villages, was along the bank of the Missouri. At the river's edge two Indian women were working with their tublike bullboats made of buffalo hide stretched over an umbrella-shaped wooden frame. A third Indian was crossing the river in a similar boat. The village, at the top of the steep river bank, consisted of perhaps 60 round earthen huts which looked like wigwams from the distance but which were bigger and more solidly built. Beneath each hut the ground was hollowed out a little; over the hollow a strong scaffolding supported rafters which formed the wall and the roof at the same time. On these rafters were laid layers of twigs, grass, turf, earth, and a final layer of clay. The houses seemed to be quite strong, for one could see people standing on the roofs to repair them or perhaps even just to chat. The village was surrounded by a widely spaced fence of stakes which had presumably served at one time as a kind of protection for its inhabitants.

In the chief's house

As they entered the chief's house, the explorers looked around before they were asked to sit down and join in the communal pipe smoking. They saw a group of men and women sitting on skins in the center of the lodge and smoking. Through an opening in the roof a shaft of light fell on the Indians; it provided most of the illumination in the dimly lit room. The moccasins that the smokers had taken off were hanging on a beam above their heads. There were several dogs lying on the ground, and even horses — probably favorites — were standing inside the house. The rest of the room was filled with all kinds of tools and weapons. Spears, bows, and shields were leaning against a post; to the far right hung a headdress for the buffalo dance, and to the left a woman's basket which was made to be carried on the back and supported by a strap around the forehead. Within the lodge, the explorers could also see a paddle, bison hides, and a bison skull.

Karl Bodmer

War paint

During the stay in chief Mato-Tope's lodge a few small gifts had been exchanged and the pipe had been passed around four times. (Four was considered to be a magic number corresponding to the four points of the compass.) In the meantime the host had left the lodge, which the guests took as a sign that their departure was desired. They were very surprised, then, to see Mato-Tope outside the hut in a completely different dress. He had taken off his bison robe (which was "medicine" for him as a souvenir of his dead brother) and now wore only a loin cloth and a few head feathers. His whole body was painted red and yellow, and a tomahawk completed his warrior-like appearance. The travelers feared dreadful things — they did not know what kind of news had caused Mato-Tope to prepare himself for battle.

Karl Bodmer

Bison dance

Out in the prairie, many miles from the Mandan camp, scouts had sighted a large herd of buffalo. At this news the whole village became greatly excited. The presence of the buffalo herd was the reason for the chief's warlike dress. The Indians did not intend to let the animals get away; in preparation for the hunt they were going to use magic to bring the bison nearer. The hunters' wild bison dance now broke out in the village in front of the visitors, the women, and the children. Several of the men had put on bison masks, and all of them carried weapons and shields. They whirled, jumped, stamped, and crept around each other in a frightening manner. Some of their movements represented those of the bison, and some anticipated the forthcoming battle. At the same time tuneless chanting mingled with the magic words of the hunt and created a certain rhythm in spite of all the tumult. Such dances were also performed when the wandering bison herds stayed away for a whole season and the Indians feared the threat of famine.

24 Bison hunt

After dancing for hours the Indians threw
themselves on their horses and raced out onto
the prairie. Their guests, whom nobody
bothered about any longer, had difficulty in
following them. After riding for half a day, the
explorers finally arrived on the scene. On the
hilly grassland they saw mounted Indians pursuing several buffalo which had been separated
from the fleeing herd. The fast, sturdy horses
were specially trained for bison hunting so that
the Indians could shoot their arrows from close
at hand or thrust spears into the buffalo's
heart. The danger of hunting these powerful
animals was demonstrated in a scene which
filled the onlookers with horror. Wounded and
cornered bison bulls had taken up the attack,
and one mortally wounded beast had knocked
down a horse. The rider could save himself
only by climbing off his falling horse onto the
back of a buffalo and then jumping back-
wards to the ground.

George Catlin

26 Indian police

When the hunt was over, it had provided the Indians with several bison which were cut up on the spot and dragged home with difficulty. The Indian village was now richly stocked, for buffalo provided many things: food and clothing, tent coverings and saddles, bowstrings and tools. The travelers wondered why the hunt was so well ordered and successful in spite of its wildness. Suddenly they caught sight of a magnificently dressed, fierce-looking Indian. Did he suspect them of wanting to steal some of the hunting spoils? It was possible, but they soon realized that this war chief enforced law and order among the Indians. He belonged to the "dog soldiers" who carried out the functions of a police force in some of the prairie tribes. They made sure that no hunter took the law into his own hands and spoiled the hunting plan or frightened off the buffalo herd. If this ever happened, the guilty man was whipped or his belongings burned.

Karl Bodmer

Welcome by the Minitari

The travelers soon arrived at Fort Clark in the country of the Minitari Indians, about eight miles up the Missouri River from the Mandan villages. The fort was an outpost and trading post for the inhabitants of the area, and every white man who traveled through Indian country was made very welcome there. In front of the stockade of Fort Clark the travelers met a group of Minitari Indians. Their chief wore a headdress which showed that he had been in touch with white people before. Another Indian had a weapon which he had probably traded for furs and skins, the most important articles of trade for the Plains Indians. The meeting was very friendly and ended with an invitation to the Minitari village.

Scalping dance

At the Minitari village the scalping dance had just begun. It was carried out as usual by the women, who wore the clothes of their menfolk and worshiped victory trophies which hung on long poles. A war expedition or attack had been successfully completed, and a future one was being ceremoniously prepared. Scalping was a widespread custom in almost all of the North American Indian tribes; the Indian warrior's ability was judged by the number of scalps he had collected. To obtain a scalp a circular cut was made with a special knife around the scalp of a captured prisoner while he was still alive. The scalp was then lifted off by the hair. Sometimes the scalped man was tied to the torture stake where the cruelty actually reached its peak. White people played no small part in the increase in scalping by offering rewards for the scalps of unfriendly chiefs. With such a reward an Indian could buy himself a gun and ammunition.

With the Dakotas

The travelers arranged with the Minitari chief to visit his tribe again during the winter. Then they set off to visit the Dakota or Sioux Indians who lived on the prairie around Fort Pierre, near the present city of Pierre, South Dakota. At this time nomadic bands of Sioux ranged from the banks of the upper Mississippi west to the Rockies. Like most prairie Indians the Sioux were not settled farmers but hunters, forever ready to move their round tents, called tepees, and set them up elsewhere. In the Dakota camp the white travelers were taken to Wahktageli, The Big Soldier, one of the most respected members of the tribe. Wahktageli was an old man with lively eyes and a prominently bent nose. He was dressed in a white tanned bison robe with leggings which were decorated with colorful patterns of dyed porcupine quills. In his tepee, which was 10 strides in diameter, Wahktageli and his wife entertained the guests and passed the pipe around. Passing the pipe was considered a special favor to visitors.

Karl Bodmer

The corpse scaffold

In the middle of Wahktageli's tent, between the bison skins on the floor, burned a small fire whose smoke escaped through an opening in the pointed roof of the tent. Light not only penetrated through this opening and the entrance but also came through the tent walls themselves as the bison hides were tanned until they were almost transparent. When Wahktageli's guests looked out of the tent they noticed for the first time a strange scaffold of four high posts beside a neighboring tent. Nearby a group of Indians sat on the ground. The explorers were told that a dead tribal chief was buried on the scaffold. The body was placed there to dry and was firmly tied up in skins; later the bones would be laid in a cleft in the rocks. This form of burial was common among the Sioux — perhaps because of the many wolves — but primarily in order to keep the dead close at hand. Later the explorers would discover a similar way of burying the dead, when they found tree graves on the banks of the upper Missouri.

Two strange visitors

While the travelers were in the Dakota camp, two strange Indians were suddenly brought to Wahktageli. Since both newcomers spoke a strange dialect, it was difficult to tell whether they had come to pay homage to the dead chief or whether curiosity about the white visitors had attracted them. One was an Assiniboin Indian called Noapeh, Troop of Soldiers. His tribe was a northern neighbor of the Dakota. His companion, Psihdjai-Sahpa, was from a closely related tribe, the Yanktonai. Both drew attention to themselves because of their especially long hair which they wore with one lock over the forehead. Noapeh also wore a striking headdress which consisted of two horns from the wapiti, an elk-like animal, with dyed yellow horsehair hanging from the tips. During their short visit both visitors behaved very strangely and seemed uneasy; soon they disappeared again. They were probably afraid that their horses might be stolen, something which apparently happened often among the Indians.

The Dakota woman

On the outskirts of the village, before the white visitors took their leave of the Dakotas, they met an Indian woman who aroused their interest. This Dakota woman glowed with a calm beauty which was accentuated by a few pieces of jewelry and the quiet but finely made clothes she wore. She had certainly done the embroidery and beading herself; work such as this demanded much time and care. Beside her walked a small girl who, it was later discovered, was not her child but came from the Assiniboin who lived further to the north. The child had probably fallen into the hands of the Dakotas during a war, and had had the good fortune to be protected and cared for by this apparently influential woman. Very often Indian girls who became prisoners were killed, while boys were more likely to be taken in a son's place and trained as future warriors.

Karl Bodmer

In the winter village

The expedition spent the winter at Fort Clark and, as arranged, they paid the Minitari Indians a second visit during this time. The Minitari huts were now covered with snow and stood in the shelter of trees. Here and there smoke from the fire inside a hut came through a hole in the roof. There was plenty of wood for burning and the Indians did not have to rely on dried buffalo dung for fuel as did those tribes living in the prairie. Some of the inhabitants of the village were standing in front of or on their huts, chatting in small groups and enjoying the weak winter sun. Several young men were amusing themselves with a game, chasing and picking up a rolling ring from the ground with their lances. This little ring caused the travelers to think that although the Indians knew the wheel in principle they did not understand how to use it as a means of conveyance, for instance, as a wagon wheel.

Snowshoe dance

Another day the explorers set out on a journey into the hilly prairie and arrived at a Chippewa village where a strange celebration was being held. Ten Indians in snowshoes were singing and dancing in a circle around a pole with two snowshoes hanging from it: they were celebrating the first fall of snow. The hunters could now slide over the snow, and hunting would be easier. The snowshoe was a large, light frame with narrow leather straps plaited through and tied to the foot. Use of the snowshoe clearly points to the origins of these Indians in northeast Asia: the snowshoe used there has a similar form. It was so typical of the way of life of the Northern people that modern anthropologists — scientists who study human cultures — speak of a "snowshoe" civilization. The cowhide boot and the toboggan are also characteristic of such a civilization.

A bison hunt in winter

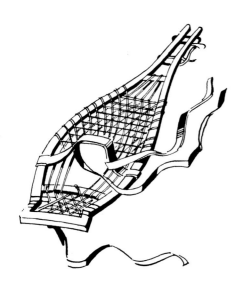

The Indians had scarcely finished their snow-shoe dance when they raced off on this simple but clever means of transportation. They were hardened runners and easily kept up a rapid pace for several hours. The hunters really used all their strength, however, when they came across a bison herd in a small wood. The presence of the herd had obviously been reported to them by other Indians. Large buffalo herds usually went south in winter but stray animals sometimes remained in the woods. Skillfully the hunters drove several buffalo out into the open where the deep snow prevented their flight. Once there they killed the animals with arrows and lances. Each buffalo brought in 10 times as much meat as a deer. Some of the meat was dried and pounded, mixed with fat, berries, and roots, and kept in leather bags to be eaten while traveling. This food, called pemmican, was nourishing but it lacked many essential food elements. The Indians supplemented their diet of pemmican by eating the liver of freshly killed animals; the raw meat provided them with iron and other nutrients.

George Catlin

Methods of transportation

The main problem after the hunt was to find a way to carry the spoils home, a task more difficult in summer than in winter. The Indians had neither wagons nor wheels; they only had dragging equipment, pulled by dogs and later by horses. During the summer the so-called travois was used to carry burdens. This device was nothing more than two tepee poles which were tied with straps to the shoulders of a dog or a horse. The load was placed on a platform fastened between the other ends of the poles, which dragged on the ground. The women carried on their shoulders everything that could not be put on the travois. In winter transportation was a little easier. After the winter buffalo hunt the slaughtered animals were cut up and the meat and skins placed on toboggans, dog sleighs without runners, made of boards bent upwards at the front and tied together with leather straps. (A dog sleigh is pictured on the opposite page.) As usual, there was something left over for the women to carry. The Indians made their way home over frozen rivers and streams wherever possible, because progress was easier on the ice.

Religious dances

With these and other interesting excursions from
Fort Clark, the winter passed, and the little
expedition set out again on its great journey
which now led them once more to the Mandan
Indians. Chief Mato-Tope felt himself honored
by their visit. He led his guests to the middle
of the village where a women's religious society,
The Group of Women of the White Buffalo
Cow, was doing a slow dance. (White buffalo,
which were very rare, were sacred to the Plains
Indians.) This was nothing at all, said Mato-
Tope, compared with the most important
celebration of the year, the sun dance. In this
ceremony, which lasted for days, the dancers
circled around a sacred post, symbolizing the
sun, to which they were linked by leather
thongs. The thongs were fastened to the skin
on the chest or back by means of short sticks
and the dancers pulled against these until they
fainted. The sun dance was a test of courage
and was supposed to give protection from
danger, but most important were the visions
which the dancers expected to have during this
self-inflicted punishment. These visions were
indispensable for they provided the Indians
with knowledge of sacred things and put them
in touch with the supernatural powers of the
universe.

Sacred bundles

It was also through visions that the young brave discovered what things were to be sacred to him. He then collected these items and tied them together in a small bundle which was often richly decorated. It could contain plants, birds' plumage, weapons, and flints, among other things. The bundle was his personal symbol and had magic powers against illness and danger. We would speak of it as an amulet or lucky charm; the white men who saw how the prairie Indians treated sick people with these objects called them "medicine bundles" or "sacred bundles." Outside the Mandan village the explorers saw two medicine poles, on one of which was hanging a sacred bundle covered by the hide of a white buffalo cow. A woman was standing in front of this shrine praying to the magic power which the bundle contained.

Karl Bodmer

The arrow game

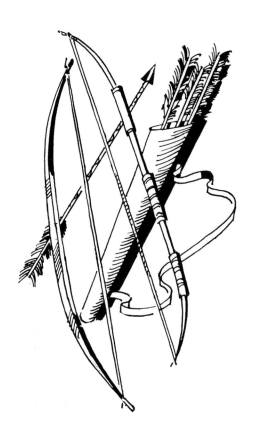

Outside the Mandan village a large crowd of Indians was gathered in an open field. They were playing a game in which they practiced using their most important weapon, the bow and arrow. The whole spectacle seemed to resemble a boys' game or the meeting of a white man's shooting club, but in reality the Indians' game was more serious and its purpose quite different. Usually it was not necessary for the Plains Indians to shoot their arrows from a great distance; in the hunt or in war they moved close to their target before drawing their bows. Therefore accurate long-distance aiming was not the most important objective in their arrow game. The main point of the game was to shoot fast and sure: he who shot the most arrows before his first arrow had touched the ground was the winner. Each shot also had to land within a marked area. Thus the Mandan's game allowed them to practice aiming at short range as well as the rapid drawing of their bows.

The Gros Ventres

The travelers followed the Missouri River upstream in a large sailing boat to reach the country of the Gros Ventres, also called the Atsina. This tribe was quite savage; a short while before they had attacked a fort on the Canadian frontier and killed 18 people. When the boat drew level with the Gros Ventres camp a crowd of men and women jumped into the river or paddled across in bullboats. Suddenly the travelers' boat was being boarded from all sides and was overrun. The Indians pushed their way into the cabin and demanded brandy, gunpowder, and bullets, in return for their skins, leather, and meat. With all the coming and going the ship began to rock, and many things were broken. The situation was very uncomfortable for the travelers.

The gloomy chief

If they let the Indians remain on board the safety of the ship would be endangered, but if they tried to make them leave it could cost the travelers their lives. At last several chiefs appeared and after much discussion and argument they got their people to swim home. One of the chiefs who remained on board was Mexkemahuastan, The Iron That Moves. He was wearing a plain buffalo robe and had his hair tied in a thick knot above his forehead and his chin decorated with blue-gray paint. Mexkemahuastan looked gloomy and dangerous, and the travelers knew that he had a bad reputation. Yet he behaved in a friendly and pleasing way, shook hands with the whites, and gratefully accepted presents. Everybody was able to breathe easily again when he and the other chiefs left the ship. The journey was continued and at a suitable landing place the members of the expedition went on shore once again.

Karl Bodmer

The curious wapiti

Moving inland they entered a beautiful area of grasslands and scattered trees which reminded the travelers of parks on English country estates. Bison herds were nowhere to be seen in this part of the prairie, but there were many wapiti. These were deer-like animals, as slim as antelopes, which at this time populated North America in large numbers, from southern Canada to Mexico. (The wapiti is the animal known today as the pronghorn.) From a good hiding place the explorers were able to watch the Indians hunt wapiti, which were highly prized for their tender meat. They saw an Indian with a gun, lying in front of them in the grass. A few feet away from him was a stick driven into the ground, with a piece of red cloth fastened to it. Soon a herd of wapiti drew near. These comic and curious animals were attracted by the bright cloth and paid no attention to the hunter. Thus it was easy for him to shoot three wapiti before the herd fled. An Indian skilled with a bow could probably have done as well.

George Catlin

The war council of the Crows

Several days later, near the North Dakota-Montana border, the explorers met a tribe which was related to the Mandan, the fierce and proud Crow Indians. They came across a group of Crows who were obviously holding a war council. The riders who joined the group seemed to be bringing the counseling chiefs news about their enemies, the Blackfoot Indians. Three of the chiefs wore painted and embroidered buffalo robes, one a necklet of bears' claws; all had long, hanging hair with feathers stuck in it. One chief was appropriately named Long Hair — his hair was 10 feet long. The Crows were prairie nomads, a wandering, hunting people who planted nothing but a little tobacco. Tobacco was a sacred plant to them. In its honor there were special rituals and a religious society for men, the so-called Tobacco Society. But just now the Crows' attention was on something quite different.

Karl Bodmer

Blackfoot on the warpath

The travelers thought it wisest to disappear quickly, unobserved. And how right they were! They were almost out of sight of the Crows when a group of riders from the Blackfoot Indians came galloping over the prairie, straight toward the explorers. A few steps away from them the leader pulled his horse around, threw them a scornful glance, and signaled to his people to follow him in the other direction. Without thinking the explorers had raised their guns but they dropped them again immediately — it would have been suicide to risk a fight. Meanwhile the Blackfoot were racing toward the place where the Crows had held their council, and smoke was rising on the horizon. No doubt an attack on a Crow camp was in progress, perhaps started by one Blackfoot warrior urged on by his family, who wanted him to win honor in battle.

Karl Bodmer

Difficult communication

The travelers were more interested in peaceful exploration than in observing Indian warfare. One of their tasks was to get to know something of the Indian languages, and for this reason their next destination was an area near the Canadian border in the present state of Montana where several completely different language groups converged. Some of the neighboring tribes which spoke these different languages were very similar in customs and culture but they were not able to understand each other; in some cases just the opposite was true. The explorers got an idea of the difficulties that could arise from such circumstances when they received a delegation from several different tribes: the chief of the Blood Indians (left), a war chief of the Piegan (center), and a representative of the Kutenai tribe. The Piegan and Blood Indians were both related to the Blackfoot and had a similar language, but the Kutenai Indians, who lived in the same area, spoke a completely isolated dialect. During the meeting there was much talking with hands and feet to assure general good intentions.

Chief Iron Shirt

The three tribal delegates had just made a treaty with the Blackfoot which ended old hostility and provided a common defense against the Crow Indians. The travelers met the Blackfoot chief, Mehkskeme-Sukahs, a polite and honest man whose other name, Iron Shirt, referred to the fact that he had proved himself in war, as well as to his leather shirt with its otter skin and ermine stripes. The explorers gratefully accepted the chief's invitation to visit his tent, thankful that the first meeting with the Blackfoot riders had ended so happily. In Mehkskeme-Sukahs' clean, roomy tent, they sat on buffalo hides in a circle around the fire and were served a tin bowl full of rubbed, dried meat and sweet berries. They ate with their fingers and found that the food tasted very good. After his guests had finished, the chief ate what was left in the bowl. Several times he had the horses checked; the Plains Indians were very fond of horse-stealing and did not trust each other.

Karl Bodmer

Pipes, feathers, and weapons

After the meal Mehkskeme-Sukahs showed his visitors a wonderful collection of useful articles and weapons. He was proud to be the victorious owner of a battle club and a kind of sword blade with raven's feathers. He had won both from the Sauk and Fox in battle, while a tobacco pipe trimmed with horsehair had come to him from the Dakotas. The greatest treasures, however, were a crown of feathers and a buffalo-skin shield decorated with drawings and ermine skins. These decorations were supposed to have given protection to the shield's first owner, a Crow warrior. However, the Blackfoot chief had managed to steal both the shield and the feathered headdress from the Crows. The explorers liked a Blackfoot pipe decorated with a fan of feathers best of all, and when he was told this the flattered chief invited them to smoke. The bowl of the pipe was rested on a piece of dried buffalo dung so that one did not have to hold it with both hands while smoking. Mehkskeme-Sukahs kept the pipe cleaner with its colorful tassle in his hair so that it was ready for use.

Bear dance

The party took its leave of the Blackfoot and, to avoid meeting the Crow Indians again, took a northeasterly route toward the Dakota territory where they expected to find more Sioux Indians. The travelers arrived there safely and as they approached a Sioux camp they could hear from quite a distance the sound of singing and drums. Once more the Indians were engaged in a dance and celebration; this time they were performing the bear dance as a preparation for the grizzly bear hunt. The grizzly was one of the most feared beasts of prey in North America. No wonder that the Indians were seeking supernatural protection and help before the hunt. In their circular dance they imitated the movements of the bears by hopping and striding. The medicine man had the leading part in the dance; he was wearing a complete bearskin and was brightly painted all over his body. The dance seemed to have been going on for a long time when the explorers arrived. Suddenly it was over. The women let out a last loud scream, and the hunt began.

George Catlin

Grizzly hunt

Obviously, the bear hunt was not carried out on foot. A group of riders followed the trail of the bear — the Indians were especially skillful at tracking animals — and led the way into rocky country where the bears had their dens. At the foot of a rock, the animals appeared: two powerful grizzly bears, driven out of their hiding place and therefore angry and aggressive. Why did the Indians choose to fight these opponents? Because they wanted the animals' fat? Certainly, but also from a desire for battle and for an opportunity to prove themselves. A necklet of bears' claws was a convincing proof of one's skill as a hunter. First of all the poor horses felt the bear claws; one horse even had its throat bitten open. Bows and arrows were fairly useless against the thick fat of the bear so the Indians had to fight close at hand. Only at the last minute did the hunters succeed in mortally wounding the bears with their spears and other hand weapons. If the spear thrust had missed the heart, scarcely any of the Indians would have escaped with their lives.

George Catlin

The medicine man

The travelers then went a little farther north into Canada to visit the Cree Indians of Manitoba. Here the explorers witnessed an appearance of the famous medicine man, Mahsette-Kuiuab, who was highly regarded for his ability to get rid of evil spirits. Mahsette-Kuiuab had himself tied up and shut into a small tent. After a while the onlookers heard sounds of beating, roaring, and bear and bison cries coming from inside the tent. The noise was so loud that the tent seemed to shake and the Indians believed that the evil spirit was in there. Then all was silent. The tent was opened and Mahsette-Kuiuab was found tied up as before. He now related what he had heard from the spirits: that murder would soon be committed, that three horses would be stolen, and that the sick woman in the camp should fast to get rid of the spirits which had entered her body. The Indians believed these prophecies and followed the commands of the medicine man.

Karl Bodmer

Before the ball game

The Canadian winter is hard, and the members of the expedition wanted to avoid its early arrival, so they decided to travel far to the south. Their journey finally took them to the Arkansas territory in the present state of Oklahoma. There were many different groups of Indians living in this area. A few years before the travelers arrived, the United States government had moved several southeastern tribes — the Cherokee, Choctaw, and Creek — from their homes to the Arkansas territory. The Choctaw Indians were famous for their ball game which was later adopted by the white people and called lacrosse. (The game of lacrosse is played today in Canada, England, and France.) The ball game was known to almost all Indian tribes but the Choctaw were masters at it. The day before the game the Indians held a celebration in which players and families from both sides took part. They sang and danced on the playing field, the players grouped near the goal posts, the women in rows between the posts. One group of players wore white body paint to distinguish themselves from the other, unpainted, team. In contrast to the game itself this celebration dance was not at all wild. To the travelers it presented a harmonious and picturesque scene.

The ball game

The game began early in the morning. A referee threw the small ball high in the air above the centerstake and immediately the battle began. Each player had two sticks slightly curved and thonged or plaited on one end to form a kind of ladle. The aim was to carry or hit the ball with these sticks through the posts of your own team's goal while the opposing team tried to prevent this and to get the ball into their half. The goals were approximately 20 feet high and some 200 yards apart. The game went on until one team had scored 100 goals; this sometimes took a whole day. Even with its present-day rules lacrosse is a hard game, but for the Indians in those days it was more like a miniature war in which a hundred or more players tussled and many broke their necks. The huge crowd urged them on, especially the women, who often sent injured players straight back onto the field.

George Catlin

Famous lacrosse players

The travelers watched the lacrosse game with excitement and horror. When it was over, the Choctaws proudly introduced their guests to some of the outstanding players. It is not surprising that the Indians who thought so highly of battle and victory honors should have celebrated the heroes of this violent game. The most famous lacrosse player of the Choctaw nation was Tullock-chish-ko, He Who Drinks the Juice of the Stone (left). When this Indian hero met the travelers, he was still wearing the traditional Choctaw costume for the ball game — a loin cloth with a beaded belt, a collar of dyed horsehair, and a long "tail" made of white horsehair. Other Plains Indians had slightly different lacrosse uniforms; the Sioux, for instance, usually wore tails of eagle feathers instead of horsehair. They also used only one stick in the game, in contrast to the Choctaw's two. (The two other players in the picture are Sioux.) The Indians often used white body paint as a team color so that the players could distinguish friends from enemies in the confusion of the game.

George Catlin

The mystery of the Arikara

The journey could have ended in the South, but the explorers had made up their minds to travel north again the following spring because they wanted to follow up an interesting fact. They wondered why the Arikara Indians who belonged to the Caddo peoples of the South had gone so far north in earlier times and now lived quite near to the Mandan Indians, in North Dakota. The Arikara had taken with them their famous skill in growing maize; it was not by chance that there was often a maize cob in the sacred bundles of the tribe. The mystery of this great migration — there are actually many like it — could not be solved even with the help of the old Arikara warrior Pachtuwe-Chte. He was very hospitable to the travelers and invited them to his hut, which was similar to the Mandan huts.

Karl Bodmer

84 The Dakota buffalo hide

In spite of his invitation the visitors entered Pachtuwe-Chte's hut warily for they knew that the Arikara had already scalped many white people — not without reason, of course. Treaties had often been broken and the Indians deprived of their rights. The main enemies of the Arikara, however, were the Dakota; many wars had been fought between the two tribes. Among the numerous items that Pachtuwe-Chte showed his visitors was a light-colored, painted buffalo hide, taken from the Dakota. Only the prairie Indians who hunted buffalo could have produced such a beautiful piece of work. Of special interest were the scenes painted on it which represented events and deeds of the tribe. Such pictorial records could amount to whole chronicles; the so-called winter counts — records of passing time in which each winter was represented by a single figure — were often painted on buffalo hides such as this. Pachtuwe-Chte gave the Dakota hide to his guests as a parting gift.

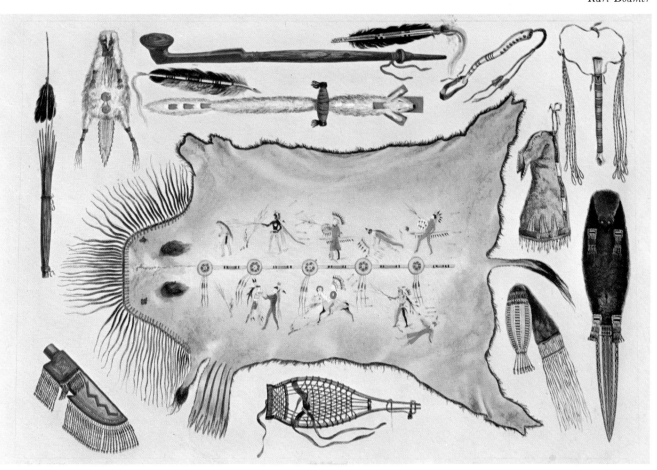

The Sauk and Fox

As it was still early in the year the explorers did not want to go home yet. They hoped to gather more information during a trip to the upper Mississippi valley. On the west bank of the river, in Iowa, the expedition visited the Sauk and Fox Indians who lived together as a single tribe. The proximity of the Sioux had had some influence on them; this was especially noticeable in the scalp lock that the Sauk and Fox warriors wore on an otherwise shaven head. Their wigwams, however, reminded one of their Eastern home from which the Iroquoi had probably driven them. These were the well-known dome-shaped huts whose frames of bent and bound posts were covered with birchbark, rushes, or mats. The Sauk and Fox were a painful disappointment to the explorers; spoiled by contact with the white border settlers, they begged for whiskey and tobacco and when they got only tobacco they turned coolly away and looked for better business. In the end they even stole a horse from the travelers.

Karl Bodmer

Flight from smallpox

Up to this time the travelers had been very lucky. They had just managed to escape whenever they were threatened by danger and they had been treated in a friendly way by the Indians, who understood that the explorers meant them no harm. The expedition had also been protected by the American flag under which it was traveling. The Indians respected this symbol even though they had no love for the power it represented. All could still have gone wrong, however, when a dreadful enemy appeared which nobody had expected. Smallpox, brought in by white settlers, suddenly raged among several tribes. The explorers took flight from the disease and eventually found themselves once more far to the north in the land of the Assiniboin, who had been spared from the epidemic. Two of their warriors received the travelers outside the camp.

Karl Bodmer

In front of the chief's tent

On the open prairie of northeastern Montana, the members of the expedition spent some time as guests of the friendly Assiniboin Indians. They could see that this tribe had very few horses, and that these few were kept for the bison hunt. The Assiniboin used dogs as animals of burden to pull their travois, the two poles joined together by a strap across the dog's back. In the Assiniboin camp there was usually lively activity around the chief's tent: messengers came and went, women tanned skins and loaded the dogs, naked children played. The chief himself — partially wrapped in a bison robe — liked to lie at the entrance of the tent and sometimes chatted with his visitors. On parting he advised them to take the road along the edge of a nearby gorge where they would be safe from attack. Thus they took their leave of a camp which offered the most typical picture of the prairie Indians.

The magic sign

The expedition had traveled 10 miles from the Assiniboin camp in the direction suggested by the chief when they came across a gorge which gradually changed into a shallow valley at one end. There they saw an unusual construction which looked from the distance like some prehistoric animal and was just as weird on closer inspection. It was a huge bison skull which had been placed upon a pile of rocks. Was it a magic sign? The explorers then remembered the clever tactics that the Assiniboin used for the bison hunt. They surrounded the entrance to a valley with magic figures made of sticks or stones which frightened the bison herd so that it ran into a narrow space where the bowmen lay hidden. The bison skull was one of these figures, a fact confirmed when the travelers noticed that the bones of many animals were scattered about the area. In bad years when the bison herds stayed away these magic signs were certainly of no use. During times of famine, horses and dogs had to be killed for food, and even so, many people died of hunger.

The Indian horse race

The explorers traveled through the land of the Assiniboin for several days and finally arrived at Fort Union, an important fur trading post located on the Missouri at the mouth of the Yellowstone River (near the present North Dakota-Montana border). Here for the first time in weeks they saw other white people and had a proper roof over their heads. They had scarcely recovered from their journey, however, when they wanted to be off again; the men at the fort had difficulty in persuading the travelers to wait for an Indian horse race which was to be held soon. On the day of the race they could see nothing that compared in any way with European horse races — no well-kept track, no meeting of polite society. The Indian race was a wild gallop which fascinated the observers by its force and recklessness. The three leading riders thundered by, shouting angrily at each other and whipping their shaggy horses. Their behavior made it difficult for the visitors to tell whether the race was supposed to be sport or a serious battle for supremacy. The winner of this wild contest was awarded one more feather to wear in his hair.

Karl Bodmer

Tree graves

Fort Union was the northernmost point on the Missouri River which could be reached by steamboat. Hereafter the expedition would travel up the Missouri in a keelboat which had to be sailed, poled, or towed along the river. The route that the travelers took through the present state of Montana was the same followed by the Lewis and Clark expedition 30 years earlier. On their journey upriver these later explorers came across a clearing in the woods along the river bank in which they found tree graves similar to the corpse scaffolds of the Dakota. Here branchless trees instead of posts were used to raise the bodies above the ground. There was no Indian camp anywhere near, which probably meant that the dead were not supposed to rest near the living. One corpse had fallen out and been eaten by wolves, and several animals were prowling around and waiting for further spoils. The wolves were soon scattered by a few shots and the explorers went on their way.

Karl Bodmer

The Piegan camp

After traveling for many days through rugged and isolated country, the explorers reached Fort McKenzie, the final stopping place in their journey up the Missouri. This fort, like so many others in the West, was a fur trading post, established by the American Fur Trading Company. It was located near the mouth of the Marias River (north-central Montana), in an area populated by the warlike Blackfoot Indians. When the travelers arrived at Fort McKenzie, they saw a group of Piegan Indians — a tribe related to the Blackfoot — who had set up camp near the fort to settle their trading business with the white men. It was the same at every fort: the Indian camp was a scene of business activity and debate but also of the quarreling and idleness resulting from the quantities of alcohol consumed by the traders. At the news of the expedition's arrival the Piegan camp grew quickly. More and more tents were put up and even the Assiniboin and Cree Indians who were camped some distance away increased their numbers. It seemed as if the Indians wanted to celebrate with the whites the safe arrival of the explorers. And, indeed, toward evening the Piegan began singing, dancing, and drinking. They continued their celebration throughout the night.

Battle at Fort McKenzie

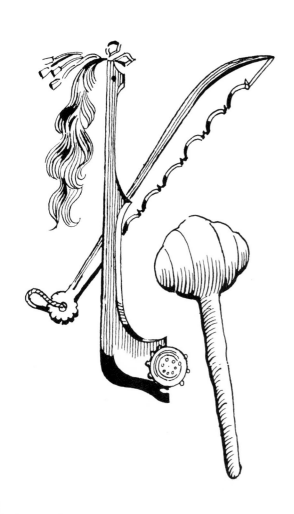

Toward morning, shots were heard. The inhabitants of Fort McKenzie started from their sleep and saw that the prairie all around the Piegan camp was swarming with Indians. On horseback and on foot they rushed toward the fort, shooting madly. Men in the fort returned fire immediately but suddenly stopped when they realized that the attack by 600 Assiniboin and Cree Indians was not on the fort but on the Piegan Indians camped nearby. It was a tribal quarrel among the Indians which was fought out with flints, arrows, spears, tomahawks, clubs, and scalping knives before the eyes of the white people. Even the wounded, old people, women and children were not spared. Torn tents were scattered around, and shooting filled the air. When the battle was over, many dead were counted. What had happened? Days before, a Piegan had killed an Assiniboin warrior and the incident had not been settled peacefully. Revenge came just at the moment when the drunken Piegan had fallen asleep.

Karl Bodmer

Wi-Jun-Jon

During the last days of their stay at Fort McKenzie the travelers heard the story of Wi-Jun-Jon, The Pigeon's Egg Head, a story which seemed to them typical of the fate of many American Indians. In 1831 this young Assiniboin warrior represented his tribe in a delegation to Washington. With the delegation he visited other large towns and thoroughly enjoyed the parties, concerts, and saloons of the white people. He changed his tribal clothing for a regimental uniform — which may have been given to him by President Jackson — and the next spring he went back home. As one who had given up the customs of the Indians he fell into disfavor and was not allowed to succeed his father as chief of his village. Wi-Jun-Jon's stories of his experiences among the white people were held to be lies, but he did not stop telling them and praising the white man's way of life. He continued to wear his uniform and to carry the umbrella which he often held open over his head as he strolled through the camp. Finally Wi-Jun-Jon was killed by members of his own tribe during a fight started when someone refused to believe his stories of the white man's world.

George Catlin

Taking leave of the Indians

Leaving Fort McKenzie, the explorers returned to Fort Union and prepared to start the long journey home. They were ready to leave the land of the Plains Indians but they would never forget what they had learned in their travels. They had seen a world which had existed virtually unchanged for hundreds of years before the white man came to North America. It was a world whose ways and people were soon to change beyond recovery. Perhaps the travelers realized this as they climbed the hill overlooking Fort Union for the last time and saw the colorful Indian camp, the fort at the river's edge, the untouched stretch of countryside, and the bright sky overhead. Several years of hardship and the dangers of an unknown land lay behind the party, and yet they were sorry to say goodbye to their eventful and successful undertaking.

Karl Bodmer

Apache (Athabascan)
Arapaho (Algonquian)
Arikara (Caddoan)
Assiniboin (Siouan)

Beaver (Athabascan)
Blackfoot (Algonquian)
Blood (Algonquian)

Caddo (Caddoan)
Cherokee (Iroquoian)
Cheyenne (Algonquian)
Chickasaw (Muskhogean)
Chinook (Penutian)
Chipewyan (Athabascan)
Chiwere (Siouan)
Choctaw (Muskhogean)
Comanche (Uto-Aztecan)
Cree (Algonquian)
Creek (Muskhogean)
Crow (Siouan)

Dakota (Siouan)
Delaware (Algonquian)

Flathead (Mosanic)
Fox (Algonquian)

Gros Ventres (Algonquian)

Haida (Athabascan)
Hidatsa (Siouan)
Hopi (Uto-Aztecan)
Hupa (Athabascan)
Huron (Iroquoian)

Iowa (Siouan)
Iroquoi (Iroquoian)

Karankawa (Hokan)
Karok (Hokan)
Kickapoo (Algonquian)
Kiowa (Kiowa)
Kutenai (Isolated language)
Kwakiutl (Mosanic)

Maidu (Penutian)
Mandan (Siouan)

Menominee (Algonquian)
Miami (Algonquian)
Micmac (Algonquian)
Minitari (Siouan)
Mohawe (Hokan)
Mohican (Algonquian)

Natchez (Muskhogean)
Navaho (Athabascan)
Nez Perce (Sahaptin)
Nootka (Mosanic)

Ojibwa or Chippewa
    (Algonquian)
Omaha (Siouan)
Osage (Siouan)
Oto (Siouan)
Ottawa (Algonquian)

Paiute (Uto-Aztecan)
Papago (Uto-Aztecan)
Pawnee (Caddoan)
Penobscot (Algonquian)
Piegan (Algonquian)

Pima (Uto-Aztecan)
Pomo (Hokan)
Ponca (Siouan)
Powhatan (Algonquian)

Sarsi (Athabascan)
Sauk (Algonquian)
Shoshone (Uto-Aztecan)
Selisch (Mosanic)
Seminole (Muskhogean)
Shawnee (Algonquian)

Tano (Uto-Aztecan)
Tlingit (Athabascan)
Tonkawa (Hokan)
Tsimshian (Pentuian)
Tuscarora (Iroquoian)

Ute (Uto-Aztecan)

Wichita (Caddoan)

Yuma (Hokan)
Yurok (Algonquian)

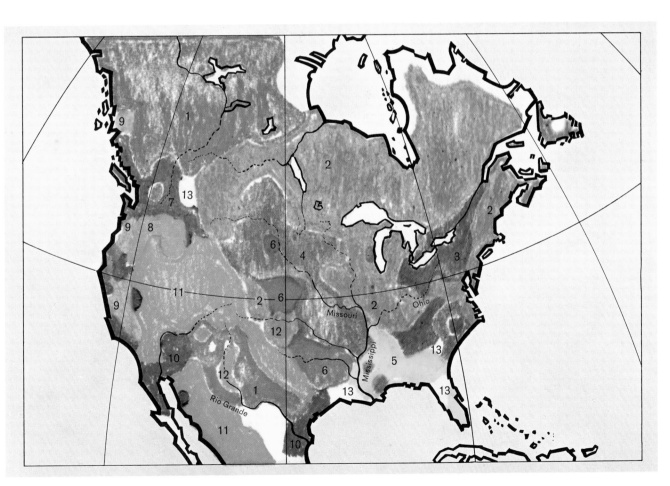

1 Athabascan
2 Algonquian
3 Iroquoian
4 Siouan
5 Muskhogean
6 Caddoan
7 Mosanic
8 Sahaptin
9 Penutian
10 Hokan
11 Uto-Aztecan
12 Kiowa
13 Isolated languages

NATURE AND MAN

Books in This Series

AMONG THE PLAINS INDIANS, a fictional account based on the actual travels of two explorers who observed American Indian life in the 1830's, features illustrations by artists George Catlin and Karl Bodmer.

AQUARIUM FISH from Around the World presents an exciting picture of the varied species of fish that inhabit the miniature world of an aquarium.

BIRDS OF THE WORLD in Field and Garden combines colorful photographs and an informative text to describe some of the world's most interesting birds.

CREATURES OF POND AND POOL describes many of the beautiful and unusual creatures — frogs, water snakes, salamanders, aquatic insects — that live in and around fresh-water ponds.

DOMESTIC PETS describes the special characteristics of the animals which can live comfortably and happily with man, including several kinds of dogs, cats, birds, monkeys, reptiles, and fish.

WILD ANIMALS OF AFRICA takes the reader on a safari with German naturalist Klaus Paysan, who tells of his adventures in Africa and describes the living habits of the continent's most fascinating animals.

These fact-filled books contain more than fifty four-color plates and over 100 pages. Printed on high quality paper and reinforced bound, these books will add an exciting new dimension to any collection.

For more information about these and other quality books for young people, please write to

LERNER PUBLICATIONS COMPANY

241 First Avenue North, Minneapolis, Minnesota 55401

Siamese Fighting Fish, a photograph from *Aquarium Fish*